You Can Play
Par Golf

You Can Play Par Golf

by
Charles Bassler
and
Nevin H. Gibson

SOUTH BRUNSWICK
NEW YORK: A. S. Barnes and Co., Inc.
LONDON: Thomas Yoseloff Ltd

This book is affectionately dedicated to all amateur golfers who are the principal contributers to golf's success, and who have made this great royal and ancient sport the great game it is today

Preface

The golf instructions presented in this volume are a condensation of the important essentials advocated and taught by some of the leading professionals of the world. Through years of constant research and experimentation under the surveillance of professional guidance, these instructions have proved to be profound in every respect.

These instructions are presented for the purpose of teaching the theoretical fundamental principles of the proper golf grip, the proper stance, and the proper swing. An attempt to write beyond the realm of the basic steps will only add complexity to the actual simplicity of the golf stroke. Many books have been written which have professed the secrets of playing good golf. There is no book that will make you a good golfer. You can make yourself a good golfer only through physical practice and by applying the principles which the professionals teach and which are conveyed herewith. If there be a secret to good playing, that secret is PROPER PRACTICE.

Regardless of the amount of knowledge you gain from learning about the proper golf stroke, it is extremely difficult to apply all these components to your physical characteristics and to conceive your own individual swinging form. You may assume that you are swinging soundly and properly throughout the follow-through, but your conception may be incorrect. Therefore, it is essential that you consult the professional teaching faculty for correction. Henceforth, for proper development, proper training, and proper correction, it is emphatically stressed that you SEE YOUR PROFESSIONAL AND PRACTICE WHAT HE TEACHES.

Acknowledgment

The name of Charlie Bassler requires no introduction to the world of golf, particularly in the Middle Atlantic states where he has won every professional golf title ever presented for competition, and in most cases for a record number of times. He has made an indelible mark in the golfing records of his native section where he has served so well, as the foremost professional, during the past 15 years. Furthermore, he is continuing his winning ways and is determined to capture one of the major golf championships of the world.

Charlie Bassler is reputed to possess one of the nicest personalities in golfdom. Ask any professional on tour, his fellow home pros, or even the tournament followers, and their expressed admiration will explicitly reveal the variety of excellent, likable qualities possessed by this outstanding professional golfer. Charlie's excellent tournament record blended with his keen love for golf and people are the contributing factors which make him one of the very best teachers in the game.

Few professionals can teach three days per week and still compete successfully against the leading tournament players of the world. Apart from winning the Maryland State Open Championship for a record eight times, the Middle Atlantic Professional Championship for a record five times, the D.C. Open twice, and every other available title in the area, he has also achieved national recognition for his excellent competitive records in the major championships of the nation. Just last year, Charlie threatened, once again, to capture the Eastern Open Championship at Baltimore, but he took an unfortunate seven on the 15th hole of the last round. He did finish near the top to win $1450. The year before, he tied for fifth and won $1207.14. In 1953 he was the runner-up in this same event.

In the National P.G.A. Championship, the blue ribbon prize of the Professional Golfers Association of America, Charlie has qualified and competed ten times and has ended as a money winner on eight occasions. In 1951, when the event was a match play affair, he went all the way to the semi-finals before losing to Slammin' Sammy Snead, the winner. During this same year, in the U.S. Open at Oakland Hill, Charlie started with a horrible 79 but progressively improved to end with an honorable 299 total and in the money, 12 strokes behind Bantam Ben Hogan, the winner. Charlie has demonstrated his competitive abilities in many other tournaments which are recorded in the official *Encyclopedia of Golf*. The question is, How far will he go? This answer will obviously depend upon how far Charlie would like to go. Right now he is interested in teaching others. It is indeed a great honor and pleasure to collaborate with Mr. Charlie Bassler in writing this golf instruction book.

Maj. Nevin H. Gibson, Ret.
Amateur Golfer

Professional Golfer

From The Constitution And By Laws Of The
Professional Golfers Association Code Of Ethics

The name "PROFESSIONAL GOLFER" must be and remain a synonym and pledge of honor, service and fair dealing.
His professional integrity, fidelity to the game of golf, and a sense of his great responsibility to employers and employees, manufacturers and clients, and to his brother professionals, transcends thought of material gain in the motives of the true professional golfer.

Qualifications Of The Professional Golfer

A good golf professional must be intelligent.
He must have a fairly complete and fundamental knowledge of the game, in order to be a good instructor.
He must be pleasant, tolerant, patient, courteous, of good moral character and neat in appearance.
He should be capable of playing a fair game.
He must possess unusual tact and a sympathetic nature to cope with that "darkness before dawn" which occurs in the lives of all men, women and child golfers.
He must be a good judge of human nature.
He must be a good organizer and especially enthusiastic to develop and hold the interest of children in the game.
He must have self confidence and determination to offset any tendency to discouragement or dispair when some of the pupils do not respond to his instructions.

11

He must possess a knowledge of physical values and trends, plus general economics and other merchandising requirements, such as purchasing, sales psychology, bookkeeping, credits, collections, et cetera.

He must know that equitable handicaps are the result of actual scores.

He must know golf rules and have a fair knowledge of the multiplicity of different types of match and stroke play competition, turf knowledge, et cetera.

He must know the value of time and of systematizing the scope of his efforts, so as to fit himself into spots which will enable him to render the greatest possible service to his club.

The above CODE OF ETHICS and QUALIFICATIONS of a professional golfer are indeed tremendous and require a variety of physical and mental achievements of the professional golfer. Charlie Bassler is one outstanding professional golfer who possesses all these qualifications.

Ed Dudley
Past President
PGA of America

Teaching a pupil after a brief observation of his swing is a very simple task for the professional, and this is the method of teaching which produces the greatest value. Faulty grips, faulty stances, and faulty swinging are quite pronounced to the onlooking professional, therefore the diagnosis for remedy comes very easy. The professional points out the mistakes of the grip, the stance, or the swing and endeavors to correct these deficiencies during the lesson. After the lesson, it is necessary for the pupil to follow up the given instructions with hours, if required, of actual practice. In many cases, certain changes are recommended which may feel unorthodox to the golfer; however, the student must practice diligently and use the correct form in order to overcome any previously learned habits.

THERE IS NO SUBSTITUTE FOR PROPER PRACTICE.
PRACTICE WITHOUT PROPER SUPERVISION IS USELESS.
PRACTICE AT ALL TIMES, ESPECIALLY WHEN PLAYING
    WELL.

Charles Bassler
Professional Golfer
Indian Spring Country Club
Washington, D.C.

Contents

You Can Play
Par Golf

Introduction

There are many steps that a golfer must take in order to execute a golf stroke. The steps required and the order in which they are performed are as follows:

1. Address
2. Grip
3. Stance
4. Waggle
5. Forward Press
6. The Back Swing
7. The Down Swing
8. The Follow-Through

Obviously, the golfer does not think of the mechanics involved in each of these steps because many phases of the swing are performed by instinct. As practice increases your perfection, the more accomplished you become, and the more accomplished you become the lesser number of things you are compelled to concentrate upon. As you progress as an automaton, the more you can devote to the difficult parts of your swing.

Actually there are only three basic steps to learn before being able to hit a golf ball: the GRIP, the STANCE, and the SWING. These entail a large volume of preparation and many prescribed movements. These methods may appear complicated but when presented in the sequence in which they are actually executed, they become very simple to follow. The complete follow-through should be a ONE PIECE SWING, but movements comprising the entire performance are broken down and classified into separate elements.

The term, "TEAR DOWN YOUR SWING," means to analyze the various components of the swing. In teaching, the swing must be torn down in order to repair the defective parts, and then put back together with the hope that the pupil can perform a coordinated one-piece-swing in the proper manner.

The Proper Grip

The essential part of the golf swing is the GRIP. The grip, which is practically the first phase of the golf stroke, is the very foundation of the swing. True, you feel certain sensations with other parts of your body in relation to the golf stroke, but basically, the true feel is within the grip.

The grip is the only link which connects the golfer with the club, and the degree of efficiency which the club produces is derived principally from the effectiveness of the grip. The club is actually an extension of the arms and hands, and the grip, which welds this connection, must be correct in order to produce the proper results. No other step in golf has as many parts to play as the grip because it is the grip that is basically connected with every movement of the swing. If you master the proper grip, your success to good golf is practically assured. The grip is 75 per cent of the swing, and when it becomes perfected, you have conquered the most important phase of the golf swing. Also, the PROPER GRIP GIVES YOU A BETTER STANCE AND A BETTER FOLLOW-THROUGH.

There are three principal types of golf grips which have been successfully used: the OVERLAPPING (Vardon grip), the INTERLOCKING, and the PALM (baseball grip). The most

21

Charlie Bassler—The finish of the follow-through.

popular grip and the type generally recommended is the OVERLAPPING. A few outstanding players have been successful with the interlocking grip, and a lesser number with the palm grip.

The Interlocking Grip

The interlocking grip is more advantageous for golfers with small hands and fingers. In this grip, the little finger of the right hand is interlocked between the index finger and the middle finger of the left hand. Both hands work together and the thumb of the left hand is not on the club grip.

Some of the notable golfers who use the interlocking grip with variable methods are Francis Ouimet, Gene Sarazen, Lloyd Mangrum, and Jack Nicklaus.

The Palm (baseball) Grip

The palm grip is practically the same grip as that used when holding a baseball bat except the thumbs of both hands are on top of the club grip. There should be more feel in the palms than in the fingers. The hands work separately. This grip was universally used many years ago but is seldom used in this modern era.

The Overlapping (Vardon) Grip

The overlapping grip is similar to the interlocking grip except that the little finger of the right hand overlaps the index finger of the left hand, and the thumb of the left hand is on top of the club grip. The late, immortal British golf professional, Harry Vardon, made the overlapping grip popular throughout the world, and the grip is now referred to as the Vardon grip. He advocated that the hands should work together as a unit, and the method of over-lapping harmonized the action of the hands.

To take the Vardon (overlapping) grip, you first place the clubhead on the ground in a normal golfing position. You then extend the left hand slightly over the top of the shaft, with the back of the hand facing the objective. Wrap the fingers around the shaft naturally with the thumb

The Overlapping (Vardon) Grip—Underside View.
The little finger of the right hand overlaps the left index finger. Both hands work in unison, forming the hinge which connects the arms with the club.

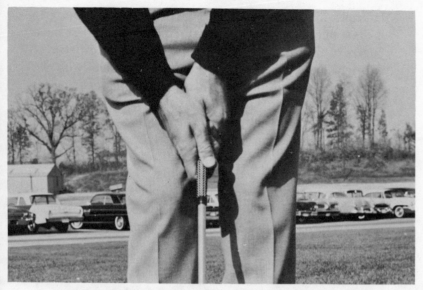

The Overlapping (Vardon) Grip—Topside View.
The "V" formed by the thumb and the index finger of the right hand
will point toward your right shoulder. Also, the "V" formed by the
same fingers of the left hand will point toward your right shoulder.

extended down and around the right top of the shaft. At
this point, the junction of the thumb and the hand should
form a "V" WHICH POINTS IN THE GENERAL DIRECTION OF
YOUR RIGHT EYE. Now place the right hand on the side of
the shaft (opposite the intended line of flight). Wrap the
fingers around the shaft naturally with the little finger overlapping the knuckles of the index finger of the left hand
and extend the thumb down and around the shaft whereby
the junction of the hand and thumb form a "V" POINTING
TOWARD YOUR RIGHT EYE. Only one knuckle of the right
hand should be prominently visible, and the right palm
should cover the left thumb.

The left hand pulls while the right hand pushes. This

indicates that both hands are working together. The grip is FIRM but not tense, with pressure points on the last three fingers of the left hand and the second and third finger of the right hand. The back of the hand is parallel with the face of the club from moment of address through impact with the ball.

Never play golf with your hands in your pockets. There is a lot of meaning in this term which, of course, refers to the importance of the grip. The grip not only holds the club but it FEELS the swing throughout. Sam Snead, one of the best swingers in the game, once told me that you play with your hands and feet (grip and stance). Ben Hogan was never great until he changed his grip.

The Proper Stance

The three types of golf stances are the OPEN, the CLOSED, and the SQUARE. The stance you use will depend primarily on the golf club and the type of shot you play. The SQUARE stance is a position in which both feet are placed at equal distance parallel to the line of flight. (The line of flight is an imaginary line between the golf ball and the area where you are playing the shot.)

The OPEN stance is relatively the same as the square stance except that the left foot is placed back, away from the line of flight farther than the right foot.

The CLOSED stance is just the opposite of the open stance. Here it is the right foot that is placed back, away from the line of flight.

The illustrated diagrams indicate the position of the feet in relation to the ball for each of the described stances. The degree in which you desire to OPEN or CLOSE your stance will depend upon the distance in which the right or left foot is pulled back away from the imaginary line of flight.

After you have taken the proper grip, place the sole of the clubhead flat on the ground behind the ball. This will determine how far you will stand from the ball. Then place your feet in a line parallel to the imaginary line of the flight.

The Three Types of Stances

The Stance Line.

The Square Stance

The Closed Stance

The Open Stance

The Three Stances and Their Effects.

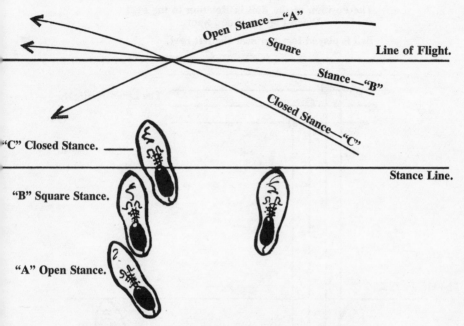

This diagram shows the path of the clubhead with each of the three stances.

Open Stance "A"—Ball will go to the right—slice.
Square Stance "B"—Ball will go straight—straight.
Closed Stance "C"—Ball will go to the left—hook.

The distance between the heels of your feet should be the approximate width of your shoulders. Your feet should point slightly outward. This will enable a full, free swing and a better pivot. Your weight should be equally distributed on both feet, with a bit more weight on the heels than on the toes.

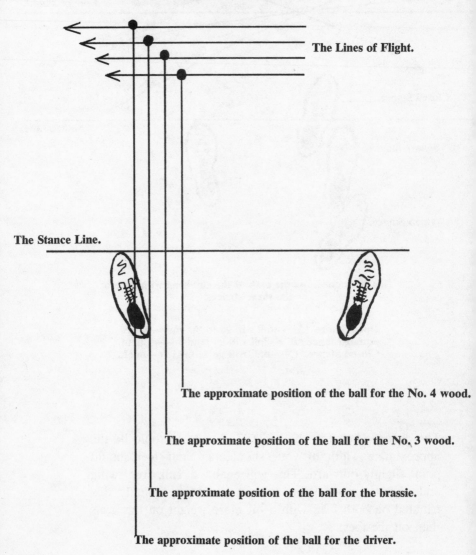

The Position of the Ball in Relation to the Feet
When Playing Wood Shots.

Ball is played forward near the left heel.

The Lines of Flight.

The Stance Line.

The approximate position of the ball for the No. 4 wood.

The approximate position of the ball for the No. 3 wood.

The approximate position of the ball for the brassie.

The approximate position of the ball for the driver.

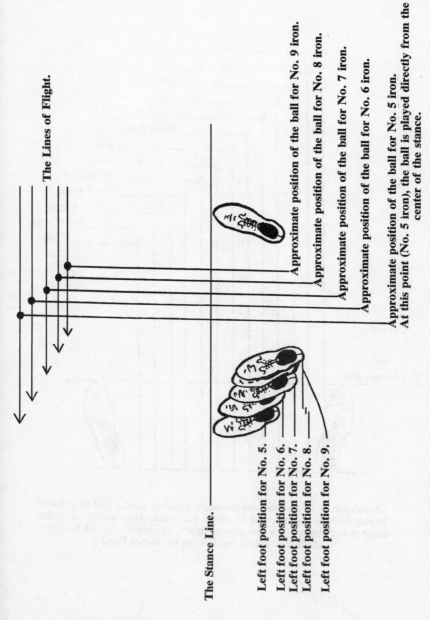

The Lines of Flight.

Approximate position of the ball for No. 9 iron.

Approximate position of the ball for No. 8 iron.

Approximate position of the ball for No. 7 iron.

Approximate position of the ball for No. 6 iron.

Approximate position of the ball for No. 5 iron.
At this point (No. 5 iron), the ball is played directly from the center of the stance.

The Stance Line.

Left foot position for No. 5.
Left foot position for No. 6.
Left foot position for No. 7.
Left foot position for No. 8.
Left foot position for No. 9.

The above illustration indicates the approximate position of the feet in relation to the ball when playing short iron shots.

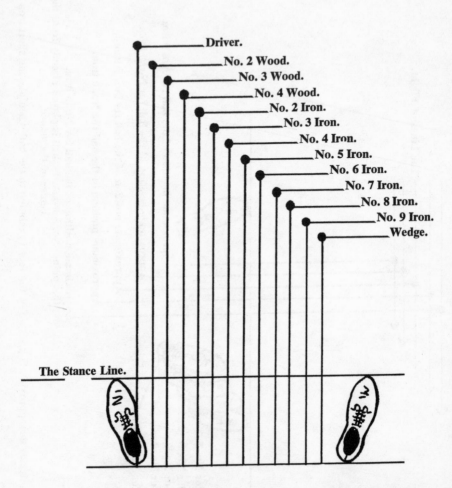

Illustration indicates the approximate position of the ball in relation
to the feet for the playing of every golf club when executed under
normal conditions. For the shorter irons, the stance would be open.
(Left foot drawn back from the stance line.)

Normally, you would take a square stance. When another type of stance is required, you should take the square stance first, then change accordingly to the desired stance. This will insure better judgment for the correct adjustment of the feet. The position of the feet should be FIRM but not tense. Flex your knees and BEND SLIGHTLY FORWARD from your waist so that you possess the feeling that you are slightly sitting down. Your stance is now basically complete. The individual must alter the details of his stance to conform to the characteristics of his physique, thus, a slight variation from the basic principles presented may become necessary.

The stance will vary depending on the club used and the type of shot required. For example, all wood shots are generally played from a square stance, and the ball is played off the left heel, as illustrated. In contrast, the short irons are played from an open stance, and the ball is played off right center near the right heel, as illustrated.

The right shoulder will naturally be lower than the left shoulder when addressing the ball because the right hand is below the left hand on the club grip. The weight is equally distributed on both feet. The face of the club is between open and closed relatively synchronized with the back of the left hand.

The Proper Swing

The golf stroke should be executed in a coordinated ONE-PIECE-SWING. However, its complete function comprises a variety of physical movements which are referred to as "parts of the swing." After you have addressed the ball, gripped the club, and taken your stance, it is then necessary to accomplish these principal movements (parts of the swing), in order to properly complete the swing. These movements are executed in the following sequence: THE WAGGLE, THE FORWARD PRESS, THE BACKSWING, THE DOWNSWING AND THE FOLLOW-THROUGH. Naturally, you are not conscious of executing each of these individual movements during the performance of the swing, but they must be correctly accomplished in order for you to complete the PROPER SWING.

Basically, there are three types of golf swings: the FLAT, the MEDIUM, and the UPRIGHT. The type of swing best suited for you is the type which conforms to your physical characteristics. Physically, the mechanical execution of all types of golf swings is the same. The only difference is the degree of the vertical angle that the clubhead follows during the swing. If you are of short stature, you should have adopted the flat swing. If of medium stature, the medium swing, and if of tall stature, the upright swing.

34

Addressing The Ball.
1. Left arm straight but not rigid.
2. Knees are flexed with the feet turned slightly out.
3. Ball is played forward opposite the left heel with the driver.
4. The grip is firm but not tense and the junction formed by the thumb and the index finger, which is referred to as the inverted "V," points toward the right shoulder.
5. The right shoulder is naturally lower than the left because the right hand is below the left when addressing the ball.

The Waggle

After you have taken the proper grip and stance, the next phase of your swing is to move the clubhead. This preliminary movement of the clubhead is called the WAGGLE. This move (moving the clubhead backward and forward) is most essential in order to execute a SMOOTH BACKSWING. During this waggle, you FEEL the FIRMNESS of your GRIP and STANCE to ascertain that it is correct. These brief preliminary swings enable you to get the feel of the club and loosen the tension of the wrists. Any semblance of a tight grip is also avoided, which in turn lessens the danger of a hurried backswing. The same principle is employed by the ballplayer who swings the bat in short quick movements at the plate while awaiting the pitched ball. This tuning up process has many good features but like everything else, it can be overdone. From this waggle, you start the backswing.

The Forward Press

The clubhead, hand and shoulders all start back SIMULTANEOUSLY as the hips turn to the right. But first, there is a slight forward movement called the FORWARD PRESS. This movement is performed subconsciously with a forward movement of the hands, arms, and body which should blend fluidly with the backswing. The backswing is actually started from the recoil of this forward press.

The Backswing

The recoil of the forward press starts the clubhead back from the ball. The clubhead should be kept close to the ground for an appreciable distance. (By placing a tee 8 inches directly behind the ball, the clubhead should knock it over on the backswing.) The clubhead should not be lifted

The Top of the Swing.
1. The clubshaft is parallel with the ground.
2. Pivot has turned the shoulders and shifted the weight to the right foot.
3. The left heel is slightly raised off the ground.
4. The head is stationary, retaining original position.

but rather should be SWEPT BACK SMOOTHLY, and then up and around in a natural arc. Your HEAD SHOULD BE STEADY throughout the swing. It is actually the hub of the swing. The weight of the body should shift to the right foot. The left arm should be kept reasonably straight and the right elbow should be kept close to the body. The wrist will cock automatically; you should have no conscious thought of cocking the wrist. The grip should be firm throughout.

At the top of the backswing, the left knee should bend and turn toward the right. The right foot, supporting the shifted weight of the body, should be straight. The natural pivot has turned the hips and the body to the right, and the left heel should be slightly raised with the exception of the medium and short irons in which case the left heel should remain stationary on the ground. At the completion of the backswing, the clubhead should point to the objective and the clubshaft should be parallel or horizontal with the ground. The path of the clubhead has moved counterclockwise from six o'clock to about one o'clock and the hands have moved to about eleven o'clock. The left shoulder is underneath the chin. This is the wind-up and the preparations have been made for the delivery (downswing). IT IS ALMOST IMPOSSIBLE TO MAKE A POOR SHOT IF THE BACK-SWING IS PROPERLY EXECUTED.

Basically, this backswing pattern is applicable for all full golf strokes. Naturally, there will be variations in the degree of pivoting with the short irons. The shaft length of a normal driver is 44 inches and the nine iron is 35 inches which definitely necessitates a smaller swinging arc with the iron shots. The backswing is done SLOWLY and is accomplished in a period of time which is THREE TIMES LONGER than the downswing.

The Downswing

Although the proper swing is a fluid rhythmical motion from start to the finish, there should be a slight pause between the backswing and the downswing. Visually, this pause is hardly noticeable but every proper swing must have it. This pause slows down the backswing, prevents the body from swaying, and enhances proper timing. Without this pause, swinging would be almost like "stripping the gears."

The downswing should start with a turning of the hips. This pulls the arms down and allows the hands and shoulders to follow. As the body uncoils, the weight shifts to the left foot. The right knee bends and breaks toward the left knee, as the left knee straightens. The speed of the clubhead accelerates when the wrists uncock and the right arm straightens. The left heel goes down to a good firm anchorage. The downswing is now complete and the follow-through, which follows after the impact with the ball, should automatically continue in the correct groove, providing the swing was properly executed.

The entire stroke should be a SMOOTH CONTINUOUS RHYTHMIC SWING. The backswing and the beginning of the downswing should be SLOW. Many detailed functions of the swing are not mentioned intentionally in order to point out the principal movements. Most of these movements come naturally, particularly if these principal and important movements are properly executed.

The HEAD SHOULD REMAIN STATIONARY UNTIL THE RIGHT SHOULDER TOUCHES THE CHIN after impact.

The Follow-Through

At impact on the downswing, the clubhead and the ball remain in contact for about 2 inches. When the ball is hit,

The Downswing.
This action shot of the downswing, taken at 1/1000 of a second, shows Charlie commencing to release that power right before impact. Bassler is one of the longest hitters in the game, and he uses the "right foot press" just about at this point, which adds more power to his drives.

The Finish of the Follow-Through.
1. The body has turned facing toward the objective.
2. The hands are above the shoulders.
3. The weight is on the left foot, which is straight and firmly planted, and the right heel is off the ground.

it will flatten out against the clubface and then bounce off the face, returning to its normal spherical shape. This contact affects the flight (direction and height) of the ball. When hit with an iron, the ball will roll up the face of the club in varying degrees, depending on the angle of the clubface loft. If the clubface is TURNED IN, the ball will soar with a left spin for a HOOK. If TURNED OUT, the ball will soar with a right spin for a SLICE. Therefore, it is essential that the clubface be kept in a square position during the most important CONTACT AT IMPACT. This is when the FOLLOW-THROUGH FOLLOWS THE DOWNSWING.

A good way to learn the correct feel of a complete follow-through is to pause momentarily at the completion of the swing and observe your finishing position. Look at the photograph of the complete follow-through. This is the position you should be in at the completion of the swing, and it is this finish that you should strive for. There are three prominent items you should check during this posed position after the follow-through. First, you should be facing toward the objective (target area). Second, your hands should be above your shoulders. Third, your left foot should be firmly planted with your weight on this foot. If these three principles prevail, you have more than likely completed a very good follow-through. By practicing this momentary pause, even during your golf playing, you will become familiar with the correct position of the finish and you will automatically complete a better follow-through.

Wood Shots

The very first club used in a golf round is the DRIVER (No. 1 WOOD), and apart from the putter, it will be used more often than any other club. When hitting from the teeing area, the driver should be the easiest club to use. The golfer is permitted to pick out a spot, tee up the ball, and swing away to the largest target area on the entire course, the open fairway. The driver is the longest club in the set, measuring 44 inches, and it also possesses the largest clubface. On a regulation 18 hole golf course, the driver will be used no less than 14 times per round which should enable the golfer to become very familiar with this "KING" of the set. The large clubface and the teed up ball reduces the margin of error, and it is with no surprise that the driver is considered the easiest club to use. True, it is easier to putt, but this requires tapping or rolling the ball to the hole, and, actually, no physical swing is required.

Apart from what has been written about the grip, the stance, and the swing, which is applicable to all golf clubs for normal swings, the principal difference for the driver is a SLOW BACK SWING. Never lift the clubhead. SWEEP IT BACK SLOWLY then up in a natural arc.

On the backswing, the driver's clubhead should circle in a longer and larger arc than used for all other clubs. With

43

Parts Identification of the Wood Clubs.

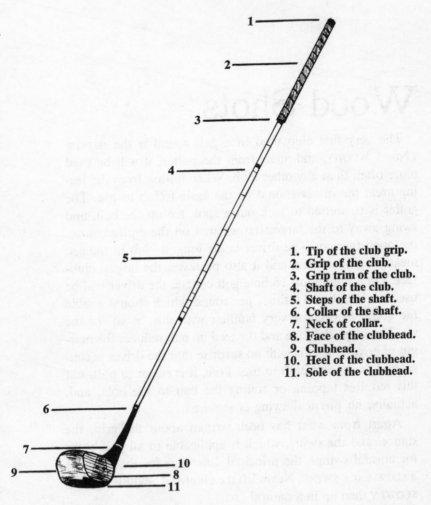

1. Tip of the club grip.
2. Grip of the club.
3. Grip trim of the club.
4. Shaft of the club.
5. Steps of the shaft.
6. Collar of the shaft.
7. Neck of collar.
8. Face of the clubhead.
9. Clubhead.
10. Heel of the clubhead.
11. Sole of the clubhead.

A normal driver weighs about 13½ ounces, contains a 10° loft, and measures approximately 44 inches in length.

the ball being teed forward, opposite the left heel, the driver should NEVER HIT THE GROUND; it should merely SWEEP THE TURF in the impact zone.

The No. 2, 3, and 4 woods, used in the fairway and at times in the rough, do not have the advantage of the teed up ball. However, these shots are executed in a manner similar to that of the driver, WITH A LONG SWEEPING EFFECT, in lieu of hitting down on the ball and through the turf like most iron shots. At times, in a tight or rough lie, it is necessary to hit the ground with these other wood shots, but this is seldom done because the proper club selection should be an iron for all difficult trouble shots. On the other hand, when the ball lies in mild grassy rough, where the grass will be between the clubface and the ball on impact, a shot known as a FLYER will result. There is some advantage to this shot especially when distance is required, because the ball will roll approximately 20 yards farther than normal. The height of the ball is not affected, but the grass will prevent the clubface from imparting the normal backspin and the ball will FLY out of the grass with overspin. This is also applicable to iron shots when hit from similar lies.

The wood clubs vary in length from 42 inches to 44 inches and the ball is played forward, opposite the vicinity of the left heel. Naturally, the position for all wood shots is farther from the stance line than for the iron shots. This again necessitates the larger and longer swinging arc and the backswing should be done DELIBERATELY and SLOWLY in order to complete this larger arc. Particular emphasis has been stressed on the backswing with little mention of the downswing. This is necessary in view of the importance of the backswing. It has been proved that a properly executed backswing will invariably produce a correct downswing, particularily with the wood shots. The clubhead usually follows the path of the backswing on its return through the downswing. Therefore, if the clubhead is SWEPT BACK PROPERLY, the downswing will more than likely be correct. Byron Nelson states that it is almost impossible to have an incorrect downswing when the backswing is properly executed. ALWAYS PAUSE AT THE END OF THE BACKSWING.

Although distance is the prime requisite of the driver, this comes naturally with a normal swing, as the specifications and the designed characteristics of this club are such as to provide the maximum distance. NEVER OVERSWING OR ENDEAVOR TO POWER THE DRIVE. Doing this invariably causes improper timing or throws the golfer off balance. It is often stated that the leading professionals on tour, and the amateurs playing in the big tournaments, power their drives for tremendous distances and punch the irons for accuracy. This, of course, is their endeavor, however, they seldom overswing and they usually maintain complete control throughout the swing. One of the most fascinating shots in golf is an excellent drive, and moreover, it simplifies the next shot.

Driving is much like putting. IT IS A GAME WITHIN A GAME. Good driving will minimize trouble and eliminate difficult recovery shots, which will definitely enable better scoring possibilities. Apart from the putt, the TEE SHOT IS THE MOST IMPORTANT SHOT IN THE GAME.

Referring again to the large target area which usually prevails for the tee shots, ALWAYS AIM AT THE CENTER OF THE TARGET AREA. NEVER TRY TO GUIDE THE DRIVE. By aiming for the center of the fairway, the ball may be hit slightly off line and still be positioned for an open shot to the green. On narrow fairways the temptation frequently entices all golfers to guide the shot. This should never be attempted.

On the subject of steering the drive, many golfers will play toward the most dangerous side with an attempt to fade or hook away from the most hazardous side. This is the dangerous method of play. Although it is not difficult to hook or slice a tee shot, it is difficult for most players to control the degree of their hook or slice. Quite often the intentional hook will become a "duck-hook" in which the ball flies very low to the extreme left with very little distance. By the same token a slice, although easier to control, results in loss of distance which could be detrimental on a long par four or par five hole. I do not advocate this pattern of play. In the first place, it requires the player to deviate from the proper principles which are taught concerning the standard grip, stance, and swing. Secondly, it entices the player to guide the tee shots which is a proven fallacy.

When distance is required off the tee for long par four or par five holes, I use what is referred to as the RIGHT FOOT PUSH. Ben Hogan made this shot popular and many other golfers have followed with success. In this shot I slightly widen my stance and press my spikes firmly into the turf on the inside edge of the sole of my right shoe. On the downswing, just before impact, I PUSH WITH THE RIGHT FOOT which speeds up the clubhead and puts additional power into the drive for more distance.

Remember, the driver and the other wood clubs will be used at least 20 times per round. Apart from the putter, which accounts for 36 strokes according to par, the wood shots account for the majority of golf shots per round. See Appendix, "Various clubs used in course of play," which describes the importance of the KING of clubs, THE DRIVER.

The Iron Shots

The principal difference in the technique of playing iron shots is that the ball is struck with a descending blow, whereas with the wood shots you literally sweep the ball off the ground or tee. Accuracy is most essential for all iron shots. The margin of error around the greens is far less than on the open fairway where most of the wood shots are played. Your stance and swing will vary with the various iron clubs played, which again, increases the margin of error.

The action of the body and hands must be SPEEDED UP AND MORE ACCURATELY TIMED with the iron shots. This is necessary in view of the shorter shafts and the shorter swinging arc. The shaft lengths of the irons will vary from 35 inches to 39 inches respectively from the No. 9 iron through the No. 2 iron.

Always HIT DOWN on the ball with all iron shots. Learn the maximum and minimum distances you can obtain with each iron and memorize these distances.

All iron shots should be hit CRISPLY with a SHARP DE-SCENDING BLOW with the blade of the club. As in the wood shots, the slight pause at the end of the backswing must prevail. The left foot should remain stationary except in

All iron shots must be hit **DOWN WITH A SHARP, CRISP AUTHORITATIVE BLOW** with the blade of the club. Body and hand action **MUST BE SPEEDED UP AND ACCURATELY TIMED.**

the case of the long iron shots, in which case the left heel may be raised off the ground during the backswing.

The target areas in which most iron shots are played are usually small and require the ball to stop abruptly which will require some backspin. There is no trick or secret in obtaining backspin. Iron shots that are hit with a descending blow will naturally produce a certain amount of backspin.

YOUR HANDS SHOULD FINISH ABOVE YOUR SHOULDERS at the completion of every full shot. Such a finish would indicate a proper pivot and a complete follow-through.

To determine the proper iron club for various shots is an important factor. In choosing the correct club, never make a selection until you have made a definite decision, THEN BE CONVINCED OF YOUR SELECTION. Indecision and doubt lead to negative thinking which must be avoided. Confidence is most essential in order to properly execute a shot.

If the approach shot appears to call for a No. 6 iron, also consider the No. 7 and the No. 5 irons. Try to give yourself a margin for error. If trouble is at the rear of the green, then a No. 7 may be better. By the same token, if a

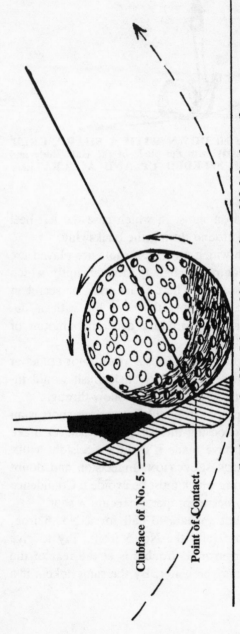

Clubface of No. 5.

Point of Contact.

Pre-impact of a No. 5 iron, which contains a 31° loft, shows the angle of takeoff and the natural underspin (backspin) of the ball. Notice the path of the clubhead arc. The club face strikes the ball with a descending blow which automatically produces a certain amount of backspin. The corrugated face of the club prevents the ball from sliding and ducking while in flight as the underspin will retain ball in its true line of flight.

The distance for a full hit No. 5 iron, under normal conditions, is from 145 to 155 yards.

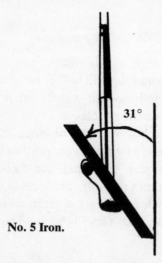

31°

No. 5 Iron.

The face of every golf club has a certain amount of loft. The loft is the angle in which the face of the club slants from the shaft. The terminology of the physical law applicable to loft is as follows: "The angle of reflection is the angle at which the ball bounces off the clubface, and the angle of incidence is the angle of the club loft." A ball hit with a No. 5 iron containing a 31° loft will soar at 31°. The chart below shows the club loft in degrees:

Putter .... 4° to 10°	Two Iron .... 20°	Seven Iron ...... 39°
Driver .... 11°	Three Iron ...... 23°	Eight Iron .... 43°
Brassie .... 13°	Four Iron .... 27°	Nine Iron .... 47°
Spoon................. 16°	Five Iron .... 31°	Pitching Wedge 55°
Four Wood ...... 19°	Six Iron .... 35°	Sand Wedge .... 57°

trap is in front and adjacent to the green, by all means use the club more likely to loft the ball. Even though you may roll over the green, you have avoided the hazard and your chances, percentage-wise, of chipping up for one putt are far better than "scrambling" from a sand trap.

I always try to discover a spot 150 yards from the green, particularily when playing a preliminary round prior to a tournament. Although markers are usually not provided, I discover this 150 yard zone even if I have to step it off, then note it by some landmark. With this information, the club selection for that shot becomes much easier.

When hitting from the rough in tall grass, just as with

the wood clubs, the shot will become a "flyer." The grass between the clubface and the ball will prevent the club from imparting backspin and the ball will fly out with overspin and with a terrific amount of roll.

When your approach shot is at a distance exceeding 100 yards, your target should be the larger portion of the green. AIM AT THE GREEN, NOT THE FLAG for those longer approach shots. Many times the holes are located on the smaller or difficult approach areas on the green which makes an approach shot to the flag very difficult. Therefore, your

Parts Identification of the Iron Clubs.

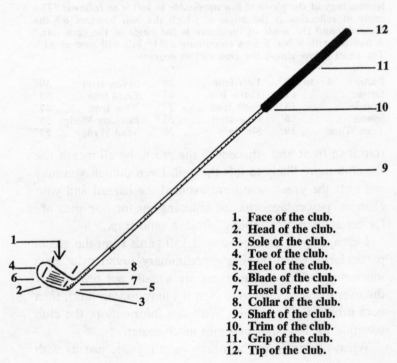

1. Face of the club.
2. Head of the club.
3. Sole of the club.
4. Toe of the club.
5. Heel of the club.
6. Blade of the club.
7. Hosel of the club.
8. Collar of the club.
9. Shaft of the club.
10. Trim of the club.
11. Grip of the club.
12. Tip of the club.

chances are much better when aiming for the larger portion of the green. It is much easier to get down in two putts than with a chip or pitch and one putt. But on closer approach shots, when the hole is far enough from the edge of the green to allow you a reasonable green surface in which you can control and hold the shot, then by all means aim for the flag and play for the one putt position.

Personally I always go for the flag, which I do not advise for most amateur golfers. In tournament play, where sub-par rounds must be scored in order to win from the other competing professionals, birdies are required. Therefore, the flag is always my target. This is not necessarily true with all other professionals as many adhere to the principles outlined in the preceding paragraph.

The following table indicates the average distances for each iron club when played under normal conditions.

Club	Old Club Name	Average Distance
No. 1	Driving Iron	210 Yards
No. 2	Mid Iron	195 Yards
No. 3	Iron	180 Yards
No. 4	Spade Mashie	165 Yards
No. 5	Mashie	150 Yards
No. 6		140 Yards
No. 7	Mashie Niblic	130 Yards
No. 8		120 Yards
No. 9	Niblic	110 Yards
Wedge	(Introduced in 1932)	100 Yards

Pitch and Chip Shots

The pitch and chip shots are frequently used around the greens and if properly executed will save you many strokes. Although different types of iron clubs are used for these shots, the shots are executed with the same basic stroke except that the grip is more relaxed and there is no body motion with the chip shot. In playing these strokes, the club should be gripped about 3 inches below the tip or top of the grip, and the hands should be slightly forward of the clubhead. Use an open stance, with the left foot drawn back about 6 inches. Your weight should be on your left foot, and the heels should be approximately 4 inches apart.

The swing should be on a straight line behind the ball and should be followed straight through on the intended line of flight. The stroke MUST BE FIRM AND CRISP with the clubhead HITTING THE BALL FIRST. Hand feel is important for accuracy and correct distance just like the putt. You should have no conscious thought about cocking your wrists, and your hands and arms should move in a one-swing movement.

The CHIP SHOT, used with a club that doesn't lift the ball as much, a No. 4 or No. 5 iron, has a low flight trajectory and rolls considerably more than the pitched shot. This shot is used on the edge or near the green when you are ap-

Proper Address for the Pitch Shot.

1. The feet are close together.
2. The stance is slightly open.
3. The weight of the body slightly favors the left foot.
4. The hands are in front of the ball.

The Improper Approach for the Pitch Shot.
Although the feet, grip, etc., appear to be correct, the important item in this illustration is that the hands are BEHIND THE BALL, which is a common error among many amateurs. This usually causes the clubface to hit the ground first, which ruins this delicate pitch shot.

proaching the hole and also when there are no obstacles between the ball and the hole. Years ago, the chip shot was played with a special club called a chipper, a club similar to the putter but with more loft and weight. Now, with the limitation of 14 clubs, a great many golfers use one of the less lofted clubs from the set. The chip shot, like the putt, is performed with the hands and arms; no body movement is involved.

The pitch shot is executed with a club that gives more lift to the ball and is used when more height and less roll is desired. For example, when a trap or some hazardous terrain must be carried and you desire the ball to stop quickly on the green with little roll, then a wedge or a high lofted club must be used. The accuracy of a pitch shot is more essential than the chip shot because the margin of error for a pitch shot is greater and if a shot is muffed, trouble usually follows because you either wind up in a trap or some other undesirable area that you originally attempted to avoid. When the chip shot is muffed, you still get closer to your objective and the ensuing shot will usually be easier. Therefore, more emphasis on the importance of this delicate pitch shot must be stressed. It is one of the most important shots in golf. THE STROKE MUST BE FIRM AND CRISP WITH THE CLUBHEAD HITTING THE BALL FIRST.

Back in 1933 when Johnny Goodman's mastery of the short game was the deciding factor that enabled him to win the U. S. Open title, the late Grantland Rice said, "OPEN CHAMPIONSHIPS MAY BE LOST THROUGH RAGGED WORK OFF THE TEE AND BAD IRON PLAY. BUT THEY ARE RARELY WON WITH THE DRIVER AND THE LONG IRON. THEY ARE WON AROUND THE GREENS BY THE ONE WHO HAS THE ABILITY TO TAKE UP THE SLACK WITH THE CHIP AND PITCH SHOTS."

The Quarter, Half and Three Quarter Shots (Less Than Maximum)

It is more difficult to hold back on a shot than it is to hit it full. In the execution of a shot within a distance that is less than the club's maximum potentiality, you must shorten your swing or reduce the swingpower. This is referred to as holding back. These shots not only require that you know the fundamentals of a normal shot, but they also demand a certain amount of talent in being able to estimate the amount of power you must generate from your curtailed swing in order to produce the required results.

In contrast, a full shot of about 110 yards, under normal conditions, would require a full nine iron shot with a normal swing without depending upon feel or estimation. Therefore, the possibility for error with these short approach shots is obviously more likely than for the full iron shots.

58

Such shots as pitching, chipping, and putting require FEEL and GOOD JUDGMENT. Naturally, it is necessary to follow the normal pattern of the correct swing, however, your proficiency in ESTIMATING THE CORRECT REDUCTION OF THE SWINGPOWER COMMENSURABLE FOR THE REQUIRED DISTANCE, will determine the effectiveness of the shot.

Regular play and constant practice are the prerequisites for perfect efficiency on these short shots. This theory has been proved by the fact that as soon as a golfer discontinues his play, even for a short period of time, his most pronounced inefficiencies will be most noticable with these delicate approach shots. An excellent method to use when practicing these shots is to select a spot 25 yards from a practice green and hit a sufficient number of balls until you have mastered this distance. Then go back 50 yards and repeat this performance by hitting the ball twice as hard. Repeat this practice from 75 yards out by adding the necessary swingpower in order to compensate for this additional yardage.

Actually, the quarter shot is similar to the pitch shot, and the principles regarding grip, stance, and swing are identical. Study the fundamentals of the pitch shot described in the appropriate chapter and apply them accordingly in the execution of the quarter shot.

The three quarter shot, which would be about a "75 yarder," is executed in a manner similar to the pitching wedge shot or nine iron shot, except that the swing is shortened. The grip and stance are exactly the same. Thus, in a comparative analysis, the only difference in the three quarter shot is in ESTIMATING THE CORRECT SWINGPOWER COMMENSURABLE FOR THE REQUIRED DISTANCE.

When practicing these shots, pace off 25, 50, and 75 yard distances and study them very carefully. This will give you a conception of distance and aid you in estimating distances more precisely. It will also teach you the proper feel and the proper swing necessary to perfect these delicate shots. Study the reaction of the ball when it lands on the green. From this reaction you will learn the precise area to aim for.

The length of the backswing does not determine how far the ball will travel. The acceleration of the clubhead at impact determines this distance. This is the reason why FEEL, just as in putting, is so important. Thus it behooves us all to strive for and develop this necessary FEEL for these delicate pitch shots.

The Normal Explosion Shot

In executing a normal explosion shot from a sand trap, the following basic steps should be accomplished:

1 — Open the stance (left foot drawn back from stance line).

2 — Secure a firm footage by putting the soles of your shoes below the surface of the sand. This avoids slipping.

3 — Play the ball in a forward position, opposite the left heel.

4 — Open the clubface and make sure that the clubhead is outside on the backswing in order to hit *across* and through the ball.

5 — Aim to the left of the hole because the ball will roll to the right after landing on the green.

6 — Hit the sand approximately 2 inches behind the ball and complete the follow-through.

The amount of sand you take (distance you hit behind ball) will depend on the distance of the shot and various characteristics such as texture of sand, depth the ball is buried, etc. Proper practice of the explosion shot will teach

61

you a sense of feel and from this experience you can determine to what degree adjustments may be necessary in order to control the ball's trajectory, distance, and roll. The sand divot should be about 6 inches long for a normal explosion. Never let up on the shot, rather stroke right through the sand.

When playing from wet sand, hit farther back, about 2½ inches, to allow for approximately five yards of carry.

When the ball is buried deep, more than 15 per cent below sand surface, CLOSE THE CLUBFACE, PLAY THE BALL OFF THE RIGHT FOOT AND HIT HARDER. The blade of the club should never hit the ball.

Backspin

Backspin is obtained by striking the ball with a clean descending blow. There are numerous theories as to how backspin is produced. Unfortunately, many players have a misconception about backspin. Backspin is naturally generated at impact as the ball flattens out and rolls up the face of the club. The ball will spin from your left to right with practically every type of shot.

To create more backspin, the CLUBFACE SHOULD HIT ABOVE THE BALL'S BASE, as illustrated. Actually, this principle is the same as if you were to step on a marble and pull your foot back. The marble rolls out in front of your shoe with the same under-and-over spin. However, unlike the golf shot, the forward distance of the marble is checked by the resistance of the floor on which this backspin slides. A golf ball in flight will have no such resistance. When it lands, this backspin will take effect and check the ball's forward motion bringing it back just like the marble.

A series of tests were recently conducted under the surveillance of the U. S. Golf Association to determine the variance of backspin between the corrugated faced clubs and the smooth faced clubs. These experiments proved that the corrugated faced clubs produced an average that was much greater than the smooth faced clubs, but by the same

63

token, a smooth faced club will produce as much or more backspin than a corrugated faced club. The balls struck with a smooth faced club attained backspin of 62.5 to 261 r.p.s. (revolutions per second) whereas the balls struck with a corrugated faced club attained backspin of 206 to 250 r.p.s. Statistics on averages revealed that the corrugated faced clubs produced 224 r.p.s. and the smooth faced clubs produced 166 r.p.s.

The speed of the clubhead in relation to the angle of ball contact at impact determines the amount of backspin produced. This explains why just as much backspin in r.p.s. can be attained with a smooth faced club as with a corrugated club. To learn the art of producing consistent backspin in degrees of variance requires hours and hours of diligent practice and training. The late Clayton Heafner once stated that he recognized Byron Nelson as being immortal during a tournament. Nelson hit a full two iron shot to a three par hole when the hole was on the front part of the green. The ball hit the center of the green, took two bounces, then rolled back toward the hole. The next day the hole was moved to the back side of the green. Nelson again hit the center of the green but on this occassion the ball bounced, then rolled forward toward the hole. Such control can only be learned through practice and more practice. But unfortunately few of the world's golfers can afford to devote this much time to their golf.

As previously mentioned, backspin is obtained naturally by HITTING THE BALL WITH A DESCENDING BLOW. To obtain more backspin, THE CLUBFACE SHOULD HIT ABOVE THE BASE OF THE BALL. These are the principles of backspin. To master the art of controlling the amount of backspin depends on the effort you contribute to actual practice. Finesse of backspin control is derived from FEEL, just like the sand explosion shot. The fundamentals can be written and read, but to master this art requires hours of physical practice.

Various Shots

Up-Hill Lie

When playing the ball from an up-hill lie, the position of the ball should be OFF THE LEFT CENTER, near the left foot. This will enable you to hit the ball before you hit the turf. USE ONE CLUB MORE than you would normally use as the angle of loft for this type of shot is increased. Your weight should favor the left side to avoid pulling the shot to the left, because the bottom of the arc is near the left heel.

Down-Hill Lie

When playing the ball from a down-hill lie, the position of the ball should be OFF THE RIGHT CENTER, near the right foot. USE ONE CLUB LESS than you would normally as the angle of loft for this shot is decreased. Keep your weight on the right side to avoid pushing the shot to the right, because the bottom of the arc is near the right heel.

Side-Hill Lie (When ball is below the feet)

When playing the ball from a side-hill lie (below the feet), play the ball off center, but AIM TO THE LEFT, as this situation invariably produces a slice.

Side-Hill Lie (When ball is above feet)

When playing the ball from a side-hill lie (ball above feet), play the ball off center, but AIM TO THE RIGHT, as this situation invariably produces a hook.

Sand Shots

When playing the ball from a sand trap or a sandy surface and DISTANCE is required, play the ball off right center, near the right foot and be sure to HIT THE BALL BEFORE YOU HIT THE SAND. Keep the face of the clubhead closed.

Low Shots

When you desire to keep the flight of the ball low, position the ball back, toward the right foot and swing more abruptly. HIT THE BALL BEFORE HITTING THE TURF. The hands should be ahead of the clubhead which will automatically toe-in the clubface. This decreases the trajectory of the ball's flight.

High Shots

When you want to keep the flight of the ball high, position the ball forward, opposite the left heel and SWING WITH YOUR WEIGHT ON THE RIGHT FOOT. Hit the ball with the hands slightly behind the clubhead and you will catch the ball on the upswing. This will produce an abnormally high flight trajectory.

Hook Shot

When you want to hook the ball (curve to the left), CLOSE YOUR STANCE by placing your right foot away from the stance line and by playing the ball almost opposite the heel of the right foot. This will bring the clubhead inside the flight line, before impact, and take it outside the flight line, after impact. You will be swinging from INSIDE–OUT which will impart counter-clockwise spin to the ball causing it to curve to the left. This type of shot also causes the ball to roll considerably after landing.

Just as Ben Hogan and some of the other professionals do, I retain the regular stance but alter the grip to produce the hook. This is accomplished by turning the left and right hands slightly over the shaft to the right. However, I only advocate the principles presented above for the average amateur as this alteration of grip requires considerable time and experience to perfect which few amateurs can devote.

To Slice

When you want to slice the ball (curve to the right), OPEN YOUR STANCE, place the left foot away from the stance line, and play the ball opposite the heel of the left foot. Grip the club firmly with the left hand. The clubhead should be outside the line of flight at impact and inside after impact. This will be swinging from the OUTSIDE–IN, which imparts clockwise spin causing the ball to curve to the right. The slice has little roll after landing and can be controlled much easier than a hook.

As with the hook, I personally produce a slice by modifying my grip. To slice, I merely reverse the procedure applied for the hook. Here again, I advocate the fundamentals as presented in the preceding paragraph for the average amateur. By this I do not wish to infer an inability by the amateurs, but this grip modification does require time and experience which the average amateur golfer can not devote in order to perfect.

Chipping From The Trap

When the trap is shallow and the ball lies on the surface of the hard crusty sand, the "trap-chip" shot may be more advisable than an explosion shot. For this type of shot, you should PLAY THE BALL BACK, OPPOSITE THE HEEL OF THE RIGHT FOOT, use open stance with feet close together, and hit the ball first. Use a less lofted club just like a normal chip shot.

Playing From Divot Holes

When playing from divot holes or bare ground, play the ball more off the right foot. CLOSE THE FACE OF THE CLUB SLIGHTLY AND HIT DOWN ON THE BALL with the hands in front of the clubhead at impact.

Tips to Correct Errors

To Prevent Topping
1. Be sure to keep your eye on the ball and your head stationary until you have hit the ball.
2. Transfer your weight to the right side during the backswing.
3. Swing smoothly and do not rush the downswing.

The application of these principles will prevent hitting from the top and outside of the swing which causes the most common error in golf.

To Prevent Slicing
1. Check for proper grip.
2. Start backswing inside the line of flight and keep the right elbow close to your body.
3. Complete the pivot and make the proper body turn whereby you are facing the objective upon completion of the follow-through.

To Prevent Hooking
1. Check for proper grip.
2. Do not let the right hand control the downswing.

70

3. Be sure that you finish the follow-through with both hands above your shoulders.

To Prevent Skying (Hitting ball too high)
1. Make a smooth backswing without lifting the club abruptly.
2. Swing at the ball smoothly, don't chop at it.

To Prevent Shanking
1. Stand farther back from the ball than you normally do.
2. Keep right arm close to the body on the downswing.
3. Keep right shoulder behind ball.
4. Keep weight evenly balanced between soles and heels.

To Prevent Scuffing (Hitting ground behind ball)
1. Keep your head stationary and swing through the ball.
2. Do not overswing or attempt to overpower the ball.
3. Keep left arm straight.
4. Transfer your weight to the left on the downswing.

To Prevent Pulling
1. Be sure to transfer weight to the left on the downswing.
2. Do not swing flat-footed; swing straight through the ball.

To Prevent Pushing
1. Keep your head stationary throughout backswing and downswing.
2. Hit straight through the ball.

Putting

The most important stroke in the game of golf is the putt. Although the use of 14 clubs is authorized, the putter alone accounts for precisely 50 per cent of all the strokes, according to par figures. The putter is actually the simplest club in the set to use in so far as the physical effort is concerned. Although the physical mechanics of the putting stroke are important, the principal requirement for good putting lies in the psychological phase. In order to putt well, you MUST CONCENTRATE AND POSSESS THAT PSYCHOLOGICAL CONFIDENCE which will enable you to stroke the putt smoothly with a positive feeling.

The numerous varieties of putting styles executed are exceeded only by the many types of putters sold. Regardless of the type of putter used and the putting method adopted, we must be psychologically convinced that both the putter and the putting method are conducive to successful putting.

The physical characteristics of the putting stroke are completely opposite from all other golf swings in the aspect of anatomy movements. The normal golf swing requires the movement of many parts of the body. In putting, ONLY THE ARMS AND HANDS MOVE. There is no pivoting, weight shifting, or noticeable body movement in the putt. In fact, the body must be motionless, and emphasis should be on KEEPING THE HEAD STATIONARY.

Just as in the normal golf swing, which is broken down into three principal steps, the putting stroke is likewise executed in the chronological sequence of the GRIP, the STANCE, and the PUTTING STROKE. Therefore, we must first adopt a way in which to perform each of these individual steps.

The Putting Grip

There are two principal methods of gripping the putter. These grips are referred to as the OVERLAP and the REVERSE OVERLAP. The overlap is like the Vardon grip which is illustrated in the first drawing of this volume. In this grip you overlap the index finger of the left hand with the little finger of the right hand. The reverse overlap has all the fingers of the right hand on the putter grip, and the index finger of the left hand overlapping the little finger of the right hand.

The reverse overlap grip has proved to be most successful as used by the large majority of leading amateur and professional golfers. I advocate and teach the REVERSE OVERLAP just as most other professionals do. The feeling in the putting stroke is mostly in the right hand and the reverse puts all the fingers of the right hand on the putter grip which has the tendency to put more control in the right hand. The grip must be firm but not tense; it should be on the side of LIGHTNESS RATHER THAN TIGHTNESS. The wrists are opposed. The thumb of each hand is on top of the putter grip and the sense of touch is felt principally with the right thumb. The sense of feel in the left hand is felt principally by the little finger and the two adjoining fingers.

Regardless of the grip you adopt, it should be relaxed, comfortable, and with a feel of confidence. Such a grip will eliminate tension and also bring about a better stance and a better putting stroke.

The Putting Stance

After you have addressed the ball and have acquired your putting grip, the next movement is to take your stance over the ball.

There are many varieties of stances, but the best stance is a position in which you are RELAXED, COMFORTABLE, AND, MOST IMPORTANT, CONFIDENT. Such a stance will preclude unnecessary tension and it will enable you to concentrate much better.

My stance and the fundamental principles taught by most professionals are as follows:

The feet should be fairly close together (square stance), with the ball directly in front of the left foot about 4 to 6 inches away. The head should be directly over the ball, and the knees should be flexed and slightly turned in. The right and left elbows should be close to the body, with the weight of the body favoring the left side. The face of the putter should be perpendicular, at right angles to the intended line of putt.

There are other details concerning the stance position that you will naturally assume, but these depend upon your physical characteristics. These basic principles are generally adhered to by most professionals and leading amateur golfers.

My stance, as the photograph indicates, is quite similar to that of Arnold Palmer. In this position I am relaxed, comfortable, and, most important, I HAVE CONFIDENCE with this stance. To me it feels MOST COMPACT.

The Putting Stroke

With the grip and the stance already set, the third and last phase is the execution of the putting stroke. This requires tapping the ball to make it roll over a smooth surface toward the 4¼ inch hole.

In so far as the physical exertion is concerned, the stroke is performed only by the hands and arms. There is no pivoting, weight shifting, or body movement. It is important to keep the HEAD STATIONARY THROUGHOUT THE STROKE.

The face of the putter should be perpendicular to the intended line of putt. The putter should be taken STRAIGHT BACK AND CLOSE TO THE GROUND, then STRAIGHT THROUGH the ball with the palm of the right hand moving towards the hole and on the putting line. The head of the putter should follow-through after impact to a distance equal to the backstroke.

In order to sink a putt, regardless of distance, three things must be done: The ball must be stroked square with the face of the putter, on the correct putting line, allowing for the necessary amount of break, if any, and with the right amount of stroking power.

These three factors encompass a vast amount of knowledge and "know how" which may be acquired only through practice and experience. Although the physical exertion is not arduous, its execution requires a skillful touch.

The essential requisites for good putting are CONCENTRATION and CONFIDENCE. Psychologically, you must concentrate to the extent that you possess a state of confidence. Every golfer possesses the physical requirements to execute a putt, but in order to putt well he must have confidence. It is almost impossible to hole a putt without confidence.

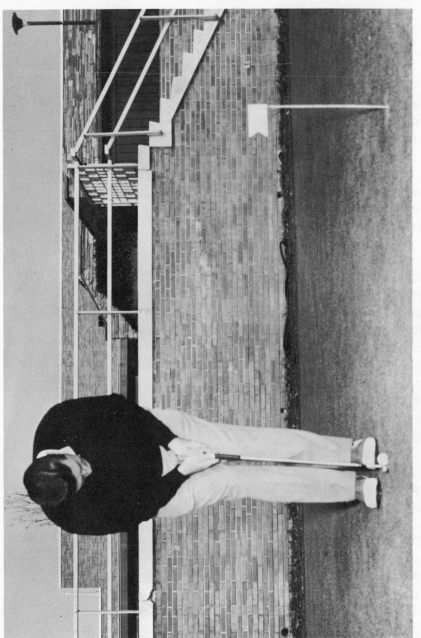

The Correct Putting Stance.

1. The head and left eye are directly over the ball.
2. The ball is played a few inches in front of the left foot.
3. The elbows are close to the body.

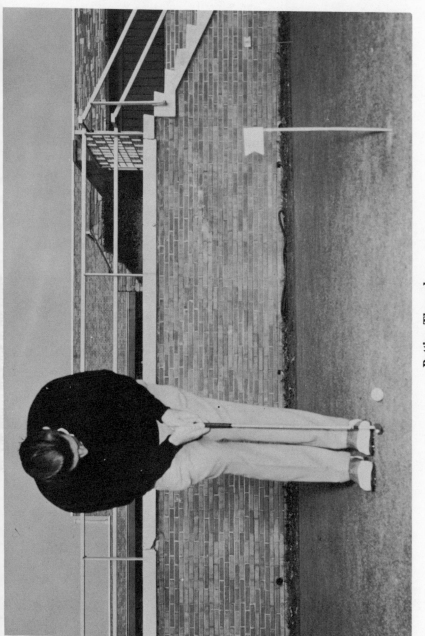

Putting Through.

1. The head remains stationary after stroking the putt.
2. The putter head follow-through should be to a distance at least as far forward as the backstroke.

A positive approach is most essential and this psychological attitude is a must in order to putt well.

Many golfers elect to TAP the ball with the putter by using a short backstroke and by breaking their wrists. This is called wrist-putting. Others stroke their putts by taking a longer backstroke and by using their hands and arms. Whatever method elected, the putter-head must follow through after impact to a distance equal to the backstroke. This insures a proper follow-through and affects an upward stroke which produces overspin whereby the ball retains a better putting line.

On long putts, it is better to LAG the ball near the hole rather than putting boldly for the hole. This increases the possibility of the ball dropping in because it also has the sidedoors to enter. This is not too likely if the ball is rolling fast. It also insures your chance of getting down in two putts.

On short putts, usually about 4 feet in length, the ball should be stroked or tapped firmly enough so that if missed, it will roll past the hole approximately one foot. This provides three protection factors. First, the ball will retain a straighter line. Second, it gives the ball a chance to drop (never up, never in). Third, it decreases your margin of error in estimating the slowness of the green. Another advantage in putting these short putts more firmly is that if the ball hits the back of the hole, it will lose its momentum and drop in. Therefore, on these short putts, let the back of the hole work for you. Obviously this is not applicable to down hill putts on fast greens which are the type of putts that should be lagged with caution.

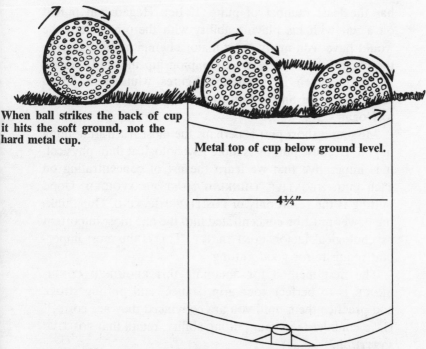

When ball strikes the back of cup it hits the soft ground, not the hard metal cup.

Metal top of cup below ground level.

4¼″

Let the back of the cup work for you. Putt all short putts firmly with an upward stroke to effect topspin which prevents the ball from rolling off the intended line of putt. The law of gravity and the back of the hole will retain the ball if the momentum is not too great. On downhill putts on fast greens, putt with caution.

Putting (In General)

Harry Vardon, the late British professional, said, "PUT-TING IS A GAME WITHIN A GAME." A player can play excellently from tee to green requiring the use of the other thirteen clubs, but if he fails with the putter on the greens, his efforts are in vain. Practically every championship is decided on the greens, and the winner is usually he who has the least number of putts. If Ben Hogan had putted on a par with his playing ability with the other clubs, he would have won many more major championships. During the playoff of the Masters Championship in 1954, Hogan hit every green in regulation figures while Sam Snead missed five, yet Snead won by a stroke. Sam had 30 putts to Hogan's 36.

Missing a short putt is perhaps the most frustrating thing in golf. Because putting is more psychological than physical, it is imperative that we learn the art of concentrating on each putt. NEGATIVE THINKING MUST BE AVOIDED. Good putting is the result only of POSITIVE THINKING. Our thinking power must be concentrated into the one most important psychological factor, CONFIDENCE. This is the most important requisite for good putting.

The best method for obtaining this REQUIRED CONFIDENCE is to perfect your grip, stance, and putting stroke and practice them until you are convinced they are correct. Have confidence in your putting ability; retain that POSITIVE ATTITUDE.

Putting practice is a must, particularly if different courses are played. The texture and characteristics of the greens will vary, and it behooves us to be familiar with these greens. This gives us that necessary feeling of confidence.

The art of reading the greens and determining the line of putt can only be learned through actual practice and experience. Naturally, the ball will roll or break towards the declivity if the green is not level. Always look for the highest point on the green. The ball will generally break or roll in the opposite direction. When playing on links adjacent to the sea, THE BALL WILL BREAK TOWARD THE OCEAN, and by the same token, on an inland mountain course THE BALL WILL BREAK AWAY FROM THE MOUNTAINS. Obviously, it is better to assume that the putt will not break unless you have specific knowledge or can definitely see the break. This is particularly applicable to the short putts.

The height of the grass will generally establish how FAST or how SLOW the green may be. When the grass nap is short (recently cut), the green will be fast, and the ball will roll more freely with less resistance than on a slow green. When the grass nap is long (uncut), naturally the ball must be hit more firmly as it will roll with more resistance and not break nearly as much from the intended line of putt.

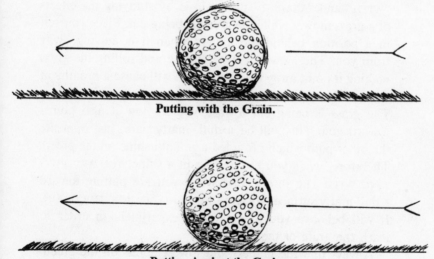

Putting with the Grain.

Putting Against the Grain.

The grain affects the speed and the direction the ball rolls. The best way to determine grain is to look for a glazed or shiny surface. This is called a shine. If this shine exists between the ball and the hole, you are putting with the grain. Use caution. If the surface is matty and dull, you are putting against the grain. Putt more firmly.

The grain also affects the speed and the direction of the ball. The best way to determine the grain is to look for a glazed or shiny surface. This is called a SHINE. If the shine is between the ball and the hole, you are putting WITH THE GRAIN, and the ball will roll more freely. If the surface is matty and dull, you are PUTTING AGAINST THE GRAIN. This requires a much firmer putt. The grain can be easily read on a sloping green after a heavy rain. Naturally the water will flow towards the lower part causing the grass to lean in that direction. This is when you can detect a prominent SHINE, and if putting in the direction of the water flow, it would obviously be with the grain.

Another excellent way to learn the difference between "WITH" and "AGAINST" the grain is by studying the effects of a grass mower while the green is being cut. Place yourself in a position behind the mower when it is moving away from you. The mower will be cutting and rolling the grass making it point away from you. This will cause a prominent "shine." Now observe the path of the mower as it returns. The grass is being cut toward you so now it also points toward you. This will be a dull, matty path, just opposite the other path which provided a smooth shine on the green. Therefore, when you are putting in a shine, YOU ARE PUT-TING WITH THE GRAIN, and when you are putting toward a dull matty surface, YOU ARE PUTTING AGAINST THE GRAIN. It will behoove you to make this experiment in order to learn the grain of the green.

Always find the highest and lowest points on the green. The best way to determine this is by using Walter Hagen's method. The "Haig" was a genius at reading the greens. He would look over the green while approaching it in order to find the highest and lowest contours, then he would study the position of the hole in relation to the declivity. Such observation from a distance is far more accurate than trying to discover it on the green. When the green is fairly level, compensating calculations can be eliminated and more effort can be exerted on the correct distance and putting line.

When the green is wet it will naturally be much slower, therefore the ball should be putted more firmly. The ball will generally hold a straighter course because it will be rolling faster and the rapid momentum prevents it from falling out of line.

Basically, there are three types of grass greens, and each type has its own individual characteristics. The three types are bent, bermuda, and rye. The latter is usually mixed with another type. The technical names for these grasses are agrostis, cynodon dac tylon, and secale cereale, respectively.

Bent is simply what it says. The blade bends very prominently, which makes it easy to estimate the type of putt you will have. If it bends toward the hole, the putt will be with the grain, hence, somewhat faster. The blade of bent grass is thin and narrow and easily recognized when it is long (uncut), and as the name implies, it will show a pronounced bend.

Rye is similar to bent grass. Both are easy to recognize and, fortunately, easier to putt on. The blade of rye grass is a little wider than the blade of bent grass, and of the three basic grasses, rye grass has the best putting surface because the ball will roll and retain a straighter line. In most cases, rye is supplemented by another type of grass which gives it durability and growing power.

Bermuda is a thick course grass with a glossy appearance and is more difficult to putt on. It is grown in warmer southern areas and its quality is able to withstand tropical heat. In the fall of the year, it will lose its green color much earlier than the other grasses, and by the same token, its green color will not return as early in the spring.

The Mental Approach

In no other competitive sport is the "MENTAL APPROACH" so important as it is in the game of golf. The psychological part of the game is by far more important than the physical part. The ability to CONCENTRATE under all conditions and circumstances is the principal requisite for playing good golf. There exists throughout the world a large number of excellent golfers who possess the physical ability and perfect coordination to play below par, but, unfortunately, many lack the faculty to concentrate at crucial times. The late Grantland Rice stated, "ALL GREAT GOLFERS HAVE DETERMINATION AND THE ABILITY TO CONCENTRATE."

The ability to concentrate is not a gifted power. It must be learned through training, just as good playing is learned through practice. Undoubtedly Ben Hogan's power to concentrate was derived through years of austere practice and training. For three consecutive years, 1940, 1941, and 1942, Hogan was the nation's leading money winner, during which period he never won a MAJOR championship. His first major victory came in 1946 at Portland, where he won his first U.S. Professional Golfers Championship. The immortal Bobby Jones played for seven long years before he won a major victory, then he won 14 in the following seven years.

When we analyze the records of Jones and Hogan, the question foremost in mind is, Why did they not win a victory sooner? They had the physical ability to hit every type of golf shot and their rhythmical follow-through in perfect coordination was an inspiration to witness. But what was the answer? We know it was not in the physical phase, therefore the answer must lie quite logically in the MENTAL APPROACH. More specifically, the lack of concentration. When these great golfers mastered the art of concentrating under all conditions and circumstances, they became immortal golfers and were a threat in every tournament they entered.

The late Leo Diegel was a great student of experimentation, and he made an excellent observation of his own mental approach when he stated, "When I have confidence, concentration comes much easier." There is food for thought in this statement. Leo associated confidence with concentration. Although both words are psychological terms, they have different meanings. The word confidence is closely allied with the physical aspect because confidence can be acquired only through physical practice. Therefore, through confidence, we have attained a sense of superiority because WE KNOW THAT WE CAN PRODUCE GOOD PLAY, which definitely enhances perfection. In order to continue this POSITIVE APPROACH we must bring concentration into play. WE MUST CONCENTRATE ON RETAINING THIS SUPERIOR ATTITUDE. Obviously, circumstances and conditions will occur which may induce us to become doubtful or even fearful of the consequences. But we must concentrate to the extent that we overcome this negative thinking and retain our confidence regardless of the prevailing circumstances.

Many professionals have stated that golf, to them, was 75 to 95 per cent mental. The latter percentage is applicable to the touring professionals and the leading amateurs. Most professionals and most good amateurs have the required physical ability and the know-how to execute every type of golf shot, thus the winner is usually the one who possesses the best MENTAL APPROACH. The man who can putt is the man to beat. This statement is proved by the fact that practically every tournament is decided on the greens. We may ask what this has to do with the mental approach. Frankly, 75 to 95 per cent. We know that putting requires less physical exertion than any other shot, and by the same token, we know that good consistent putting is based principally on our confidence and concentration. Therefore, the man who putts well is the man who has the correct mental approach; he is the man to beat.

You may be equal to your opponent in the physical sense, yet he may defeat you in a match, psychologically. Walter Hagen, reputed as the greatest match player in the game, possessed no special talent in the physical mechanics, yet he crucified his contemporaries psychologically. He retained a superior mental approach which enabled him to win a record number of five U.S. Professional Golfers Championship (match play) titles, and a total of eleven MAJOR titles, which is the professional world record. Yet, one of the strangest things about the "Haig" was his erratic physical play. He would invariably miss several shots during a round and on almost every occasion he would produce a brilliant recovery shot. Such a performance would obviously rouse the strongest competitors to some degree. Imagine, a great professional completely "dubbing" a shot, then, with confidence and concentration, producing a marvelous shot while under intense fire.

Recently a match was surveyed where player A hit 15 greens in regulation figures and scored a 76. His opponent, player B, hit nine greens and scored a winning 75. From a statistical viewpoint (from tee to green) A physically played for an 83.25 per cent average while B physically played for a 50 per cent average. This should present an excellent conception of the value of the MENTAL APPROACH. Although putting is half the game, the physical requirements are practically nil. To further analyze this match, A should have scored no more than 7 per cent, three over par, in light of his physical play, while B should have scored no more than an 81, nine over par. Yet A went OVER his quota by one while B overcame his physical deficiencies and scored six UNDER his physical play. This match, like many others, was not won physically, but rather mentally. The winner had the proper MENTAL APPROACH. More specifically, he had CONFIDENCE AND CONCENTRATION.

Robert Tyre Jones Jr., the great immortal, once said, "There are two kinds of golf, GOLF AND TOURNAMENT GOLF, and they are not at all the same." Bobby did not explain in detail the difference between the two, but we can ascertain that the difference is definitely in the psychological part and thus could well be CONCENTRATION. The vast majority of golfers have a tendency to "tighten up" while under pressure. This is not abnormal; it is almost a natural consequence. But there are those who HAVE TRAINED themselves to CONCENTRATE AGAINST NEGATIVE THINKING. Failing to produce the proper shot under pressure, "choking up," is commonly caused by negative thinking. WE MUST THINK IN THE POSITIVE SENSE. The best way to retain confidence is to CONCENTRATE ON BEING CONFIDENT. Without this concentration we lose our confidence and naturally our performance of play is far below our potentiality in the physical sense.

Many outstanding golfers have confined their concentration to one individual pattern with a great degree of success. They have only one objective in mind, and that is to beat "ole man par." Whether in stroke play or against opponents in match play, the objective remains the same. It is reasonable to assume that the MENTAL APPROACH will be much easier if we confine our concentration to the subject of par rather than to the entire field of competitors. "Ole man par" never moves; he is always there and at times he plays very difficult, depending on the weather, condition of the course, etc. There is great satisfaction in defeating "ole man par" and even though we may lose our match, there is no bitterness when we have given "ole man par" a fair struggle. After all, our original concern was to PLAY PAR GOLF.

As often stated, this concentration does not come easy. The late Babe Zaharias once stated that with every practice shot she executed, she mentally assumed that it was for a championship title. Such psychological training, in conjunction with physical practice, undoubtedly contributed to the Babe's great golfing record.

In 1945, when Byron Nelson accummulated numerous golf records, I had the pleasure of seeing him score a record 259 for 72 holes at the Boardmoor Golf Club in Seattle. In the third round, Nelson fired a 63, and on a number of occasions during his actual swing, a terrific roar would ring out from the crowds at the nearby Washington University football stadium. When Nelson finished, I asked him if this noise had interfered, and he replied, "WHAT NOISE."

Lord Byron's ability to maintain complete mental control under such adverse circumstances is indeed a great psychological achievement and which again substantiates the importance of CONCENTRATION. It is reputed that Byron Nelson's concentration was so predominant that he was almost in a state of hypnotism while playing in competition.

Recently, at the Masters Tournament, Gene Sarazen commented that he was hitting the ball as far and as straight as ever, although his winless streak was contributed to the fact that he was unable to concentrate during an entire 72 hole grind. Gene further stated that it was difficult to maintain top concentrating stamina over a long period of time. After pursuing the game of championship golf for over 40 years, and in such pageantry fashion, the "Little Squire" has no qualms.

A pronounced endeavor has been made to emphasize the value of the psychological side of golf. We are not advocating that a person should practice less. On the contrary, proper practice under the surveillance and guidance of competent golf professionals is essential in order to master the game with some degree of proficiency. The fundamentals of playing golf are rather easy and to play a fair game is not difficult, if the individual is determined and will devote time for proper instruction and practice. However, to play good, consistent golf you must be a determined individual who is ready to make a sincere effort to practice. The calibre of your golf is primarily based on the effort you exert in practice. THAT is PROPER PRACTICE.

Suppose you take the game seriously and you practice to the extent that you can play any shot, including difficult trouble shots. Such determination has enabled you to master the game physically. But can you produce these shots under all circumstances and under all conditions? This is where

THE MENTAL APPROACH plays such an important role. Up
to this point you have exercised certain psychological as-
pects which are combined with the physical part of the
game. As an example, you have become a DETERMINED
golfer, and you have gained a tremendous amount of CON-
FIDENCE as a result of proper practice from which you have
achieved the ability to execute all types of shots. In fact, you
even possess a positive attitude; a most important ingredient
in WINNING GOLF. But there is just one more psychological
factor which must be considered, CONCENTRATION. This
latter part of the mental approach to good golf is required. It
allows you to retain your confidence and to produce the type
of play commensurate with your physical ability, UNDER
ALL CIRCUMSTANCES AND CONDITIONS.

Examples of Jones, Hagan, Nelson, Hogan, and a host
of other immortal golfers have been presented in order to
explain various psychological facts. The reader may wonder
how he or she fits into a picture with such golfing celebrities.
You may rest assured that the principles contained in this
section, "THE MENTAL APPROACH," are applicable to all
golfers, whether they play frequently or otherwise.

The association of brains and golf is not new. It began
with the origin of this ancient sport, but today few golfers
realize the importance of the psychological side of golf. Of
the latest 975 golf books that have been written only 19
books have attempted to emphasize the significance of the
mental side. The others describe the physical requirements.

The physical movements of our muscles are controlled
by our minds. Therefore, EVERY GOLF SWING IS CONTROLLED
BY THE PSYCHOLOGICAL SENSES. It is an accepted fact that
the mind functions most rapidly in low resistance paths.
Thus, we must train our minds to concentrate in order to
avoid these undesirable paths. When we concentrate, we

are merely setting our mental machinery toward some definite objective. Only by proper concentration are we able to stave off negative thinking which inevitably leads to inferior complexes and loss of confidence.

When we think in a POSITIVE manner, we usually produce accordingly, and when we do we are exercising the functions of two principal psychological terms, CONFIDENCE AND CONCENTRATION. The proper mental approach, which embraces these two terms, is required so that we can produce the type of golf play which is equal to our physical potentialities. When we have achieved this, we have mastered the most important phase of playing high calibre golf.

Appendix

Golf Ball Specifications

The standard golf ball, as approved for play in the United States by the U. S. Golf Association, weighs 1.620 ounces and measures 1.680 inches in diameter. These requirements, plus other specifications, are imposed on the golf ball manufacturers. Basically there are two principal types of golf balls. There is the highly compressed, "HARD" ball, and the low compressed, "SOFT" ball. The principal difference is that the hard ball is produced by increasing the rubber tensile as the ball is being wound. The soft ball is wound with less tightness which obviously makes it softer. Other differences exist in the various types of covers and cores used for each of the balls.

The distance a ball travels is determined first by the amount it is compressed on the clubface at impact, and second by the amount of energy built into the ball. Thus, in comparison, if both balls were "flattened" against the clubface in a similar manner the hard ball would rebound farther. However, it takes far greater clubhead speed and squarer contact to compress the harder, more tightly wound ball. The soft ball, wound less tightly, can be compressed

93

The illustration below indicates the approximate distance and flight trajectory of a golf ball when hit by various iron clubs under normal conditions.

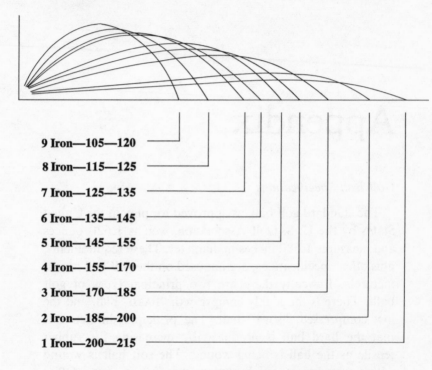

9 Iron—105—120

8 Iron—115—125

7 Iron—125—135

6 Iron—135—145

5 Iron—145—155

4 Iron—155—170

3 Iron—170—185

2 Iron—185—200

1 Iron—200—215

with less clubhead speed and a slightly off-center hit. The thin cover of a hard ball will cut easily when only slightly topped, whereas the tough cover on the soft ball can endure a lot of punishment.

For the average golfer and for the golfer who swings with less clubhead speed, the low compression ball is better to use. These balls are designed for durability, and they will decrease the margin of error. The hard balls are designed for the professionals and good amateur players who consistently hit the ball square with a lot of power. The GOLF

PROFESSIONAL who is familiar with your game should be consulted in this connection. He is the best authority for advising you on the type of ball best suited for your game.

A ball performs better at about 85 degrees and it will travel from 10 to 20 yards farther than a cold ball. When playing in cold weather, you should change balls on every tee. Under such conditions it will be to your advantage to carry three balls in your pocket close to the warmth of your body and to change to a warm, dry ball on every tee. A spot of water between clubface and ball makes a lot of difference in the way the ball bounces off the face of the club. During recent years, handwarmers and golf-ball warmers have become very popular.

Golf ball manufacturers are controlled by the U.S.G.A. in regards to specifications. This control must be exercised in order to preclude the production of distance balls, which in turn would make the golf courses obsolete in the aspect of regulating the standard par figures. A golf ball that travels faster than 174 miles per hour is exceeding the official limit of the U.S.G.A.

Types Of Club Shafts

There are five principal types of club shafts that are divided into various series which define the specific stiffness or flexibility of the club shafts. The five types and the classification of golfers in which each are designed, follows:

L or No. 4 — The most flexible shaft of all. Designed for most women and older men players.
A or No. 3 — The medium flexible shaft used by strong women and light hitting men players.
R or No. 2 — The medium stiff shaft. Average and suitable for most men players.

S or No. 1 — The stiff or firm shaft. Designed for normal power
                   hitters.
X   — The extra stiff shaft. Designed for extra powerful
                   hitters.

The subject of swing-weight, shaft-flex, overall weight,
and length of the golf clubs, has many facets and to the average player is quite complicated. When selecting your
golf clubs, CONSULT YOUR GOLF PROFESSIONAL. He knows
precisely the club specifications that most conform to your
physique and golf swing. Just like the doctor who makes a
diagnosis and then writes out a medical prescription for
your ailment, the golf professional does the same thing in
the matter of prescribing the proper golf clubs most suitable for you. Golf is the professional's job. He teaches it,
studies it, lives it, and even sleeps with it. Without utilizing
his assistance, you will be depriving yourself of many
valuable advantages.

Swingweights

Swingweight is a calibration of the energy factor in swinging the head of the club to match one club with the other.
   Prior to the introduction of steel shafts, clubs were classified by dead weight (total weight of the club). The flexibility of the shaft could be increased by paring down the
hickory shafts until the desired whip was obtained. This
greater flexibility made the club feel heavy even though it
was lighter in total weight. It was at this point that the con-
cept of swingweight was begun. The manufacturers employed scientists to study this subject and these scientists
immediately revealed that the point of percussion became
lower when the club shaft was lightened. We also learned
that energy equals mass times velocity squared and if you
doubled the mass and retained the speed you doubled the

power. If you doubled the speed and retained the mass you quadrupled the power. Thus came the complexity of this swingweight business.

The following chart indicates the most common swing-weight nomenclatures which are designed for various types of players:

C-6 to C-8 — For players hitting about 160 yards
C-8 to D-1 — For players hitting about 185 yards
D-1 to D-3 — For players hitting about 210 yards
D-3 to D-5 — For players hitting about 225 yards
D-5 to E-0 — For extra powerful hitters who average over 235 yards.

Naturally the professional should be consulted before clubs are acquired. He will know the precise swingweight which is best suited for your swing.

Par Defined

The United States Golf Association states that, "Par means perfect play without flukes and under ordinary weather conditions, always allowing two strokes on each putting green." The Association has published a chart as a means by which golf courses may determine the correct par figures. The directions for computing par based on the length of holes is as follows:

Men's Par
Par 3 — Up to 250 yards, inclusive.
Par 4 — 251 to 470 yards, inclusive.
Par 5 — 470 to 600 yards, inclusive.
Par 6 — 600 yards and over. (No Provision)

Women's Par
Par 3 — Up to 210 yards, inclusive.
Par 4 — 211 to 400 yards, inclusive.
Par 5 — 401 to 575 yards, inclusive.
Par 6 — 576 yards and over. (No Provision)

Club Specifications Of The Leading Pros

PROFESSIONAL	AGE	HGHT	WT	DRIVER LENGTH	DRIVER WT OZ	SWING WEIGHT	SHAFT FLEX
Jerry Barber	45	5′5″	137	43″	13¼	D-6	Stiff (S)
Charlie Bassler	39	6′½″	185	44″	13½	D-2	Stiff (S)
George Bayer	37	6′5″	240	44″	14⅛	E-0	X-Stiff (X)
Tommy Bolt	42	6′	170	44″	13¾	D-5	Stiff (S)
Jack Burke	39	5′9″	165	43″	13½	D-2	Stiff (S)
Walter Burkemo	44	5′9½″	172	43½″	14	D-5	Stiff (S)
Jacky Cupit	23	5′9″	170	43½″		D-3	Stiff (S)
Jack Fleck	40	5′11″	165	44″	13½	D-4	Stiff (S)
Doug Ford	40	5′10″	180	43½″	14 5/16	D-4½	X-Stiff (X)
Bob Goalby	32	6″	195	43″	13⅝	D-4	Stiff (S)
Paul Harney	34	5′11″	142	43½″	13½	D-4	Stiff (S)
Ted Kroll	44	5′8½″	152	43″		D-6	Stiff (S)
Gene Littler	33	5′9½″	167	43″	13½	D-3	Stiff (S)
Lloyd Mangrum	49	6′	160	43½″	14	D-8	Stiff (S)
Cary Middlecoff	41	6′2″	185	43⅞″	13¼	D-8	X-Stiff (X)
Jack Nicklaus	22	5′11″	170	43″		D-1	Stiff (S)
Arnold Palmer	33	5′11″	170	43½″	13 11/16	D-0	A-Stiff (X)
Gary Player	27	5′7″	150	44″	14	D-7	Stiff (S)
Bob Rosburg	36	5′11″	195	44″	13⅝	D-3	Stiff (S)
Mason Rudolph	28	5′11″	180	43″	14	D-6	Stiff (S)
Doug Sanders	29	5′10½″	160	43″	13⅜	D-3	M-Stiff (R)
Sam Snead	50	5′11″	182	43½″	13 7/16	D-6	X-Stiff (X)
Mike Souchak	35	5′11″	200	43″		D-9	X-Stiff (X)
Art Wall	38	6′	165	43″	13 3/16	D-3	Stiff (S)
Don Whitt	33	5′10″	150	43¼″		D-5	Stiff (S)

(The above statistics supplied by GOLF DIGEST)

The United States Golf Association points out that the above figures are not arbitrary, because some allowance should be made for the configuration of the ground and any other difficult or unusual conditions. Due consideration should be given the severity of the hazards, especially on a hole where par is doubtful. Each hole should be measured horizontally from the center of the tee to the center of the green, following the planned line of play.

The word, "bogey," originated in England by Hugh Rotherham of Coventry, and it represented the score in which a scratch player took on each hole. Now the term is generally used as one over par.

A regulation par 72 golf course, according to USGA standards, comprises 18 holes which are rated with specified par figures and distances which follow:

Holes	Par	Strokes	Minimum & Maximum Distance (Men)
10	4	40	251 to 470 yards
4	5	20	470 to 600 yards
4	3	12	Up to 250 yards
Totals 18	72	72	(6600 yard average)

The following statistics indicate the number of times you will use various golf clubs in order to play the course in par, without flukes.

Club	Total Times Used	Total Strokes Required
(1) Putter	36	36
(2) Wood Clubs	20	20
(3) Iron Clubs	16	16
Total	72	72

(1) Putter — Two putts for each of the 18 greens — total 36 strokes.

(2) Wood Clubs — At least 14 with driver for tee shots on the par 4 & 5 holes. Four woods for the second shot on the four par 5 holes and usually two woods for two of the par 3's.

(3) Iron Clubs — Ten approaches for the par 4 holes and four for
the par 5 holes and usually two for the par 3
holes.

Two of the par three holes are usually long enough to require a wood shot for the average golfer.

The above data is illustrated primarily to show the importance of the driver and the wood shots. Apart from the putter, the driver will be used more than any other club, and the efficiency in which it is used will generally gauge the calibre of golf you play.

Shifting Weight

Contrary to accepted theory, there is more weight on the right foot, AT IMPACT than on the left foot. The average touring professional, using a driver, shifts only 47.25 per cent of his weight to the left foot at impact. The percentage is even less with iron shots. At the completion of the swing, 69.77 per cent of the weight is shifted to the left with the driver, and a more definite 81.12 per cent with the iron.

These statistics, which came as a great surprise to the large majority of the touring professionals, were discovered through a study conducted by Mrs. Nanette McIntyre and Dr. Raymond Snyder of U.C.L.A.'s physical education department during the 1962 Los Angeles Open. Thirty touring professionals took part in this experiment and each swung six times. A movie camera, 16mm driven at 64 frames per second, recorded the action. The no-spring Toledo scales were installed underground and collaborated to reflect the indicated weight transfer. Hysterisis and kinetic factors were taken into account which proved the recordings to be precisely correct.

Knowledge of this data will not necessarily improve our

golf swing. However, it does prove one thing. When the swing is properly executed with the proper pivot, the percentage of actual weight shifting is small. When we fail to pivot and sway with the swing, the percentage of weight shifting is greater. Power is not generated from body weight, but rather from good posture and balance and proper timing. It is reasonable to assume that a swing can be more accurately timed and controlled with the least amount of weight shift.

The average distribution of weight at various positions during swing, follows. This data was compiled by *Golf Digest*.

Figures are percentages which represent that portion of the average subject's total body weight.

Driver

	Right	Left
1 - At address	48.06	51.94
2 - Forward press	42.09	57.91
3 - Top of backswing	70.77	29.23
4 - Impact	52.75	47.25
5 - After impact	49.95	50.05
6 - Finish	30.23	69.77

Average Percentage Of Weight Shifts

A - To left on forward press	5.97
B - To right on backswing	28.68
C - To left on downswing	18.02
D - To left on follow-through	22.52

Eight (8) Iron

	Right	Left
1 - At address	47.66	52.34
2 - Forward press	42.40	57.60
3 - Top of backswing	68.18	31.82
4 - Impact	55.87	44.13
5 - After impact	53.00	47.00
6 - Finish	18.88	81.12

Average Percentage Of Weight Shifts

A - To left on forward press 5.26
B - To right on backswing 25.78
C - To left on downswing 12.31
D - To left on follow-through 36.99

Average percentage of total weight shifted to left from top of the backswing to finish: Driver—40.54 Eight (8) Iron—49.30.

The preceding statistics on shifting weight is given as a matter of interest and should not be interpreted to indicate that the weight is not shifted from the right to the left during follow-through. These facts refer principally to percentages of total weight shifted during certain movements of the swing. Keep in mind that 69.77 per cent of the weight is on the left side at the finish of the swing with the driver and with an eight iron shot, 81.12 per cent is on the left at the finish.